WITHDRAWN

NOTHINGNESS

By Alan Watts

Book III in the Illustrated Series
THE ESSENCE OF ALAN WATTS

ALAN WATTS " . . . in *Nothingness*, has provided a wonderful somethingness. . . ."
—Laura Huxley

Photographs by Joseph McHugh

CELESTIAL ARTS
Millbrae, California

Copyright © 1974 by Celestial Arts
231 Adrian Road, Millbrae, California 94030

No part of this book may be reproduced by any
mechanical, photographic, or electronic process,
or in the form of a phonographic recording, nor may it
be stored in a retrieval system, transmitted, or
otherwise copied for public or private use without the
written permission of the publisher.

First Printing, July 1974
Made in the United States of America

Cover photo of Alan Watts by Margo Moore

Collected Series Library of Congress No. 74-10124

Library of Congress Cataloging in Publication Data

Watts, Alan Wilson, 1915–1973
   Nothingness.

   (His The Essence of Alan Watts, v. 3)

   1. Nothing (Philosophy)   I. Title.
B945.W321   1974   vol. 3 (B945.W323) 191s (111) 74-13650
ISBN 0-912310-77-4

THE STORY OF ALAN WATTS

For more than twenty years Alan Watts earned a reputation as the foremost interpreter of Eastern philosophies to the West. Beginning at the age of 20, when he wrote *The Spirit of Zen*, he developed an audience of millions who were enriched by his offerings through books, tape recordings, radio, television, and public lectures.

He wrote 25 books, each building toward a personal philosophy that he shared, in complete candor and joy, with his readers and listeners throughout the world. They presented a model of individuality and self-expression that can be matched by few contemporaries. His life and work reflect an astonishing adventure: he was editor, Anglican priest, graduate dean, broadcaster, and author-lecturer. He had fascinations for cooking, calligraphy, singing, and dancing. He held fellowships from Harvard University and the Bollingen Foundation and was Episcopal Chaplain at Northwestern University. He became professor and dean of the American Academy of Asian Studies in San Francisco, made the television series "Eastern Wisdom and Modern Life" for National Educational Television, and served as visiting consultant to many psychiatric institutes and hospitals. He traveled widely with students in Japan.

Born in England in 1915, Alan Watts attended King's School Canterbury, served on the Council of the World Congress of Faiths (1936–38), and came to the United States in 1938. He held a Master's Degree in Theology from Seabury-Western Theological Seminary and an Honorary D.D. from the University of Vermont in recognition of his work in Comparative Religion.

Alan Watts died in 1973. *The Essence of Alan Watts*, a series of nine books in the unique *Celestial Arts* format, includes edited transcripts by his wife Mary Jane Watts of videotaped lectures that were produced by his friend, Henry Jacobs, and filmed by his son, Mark Watts, in the last years of his life.

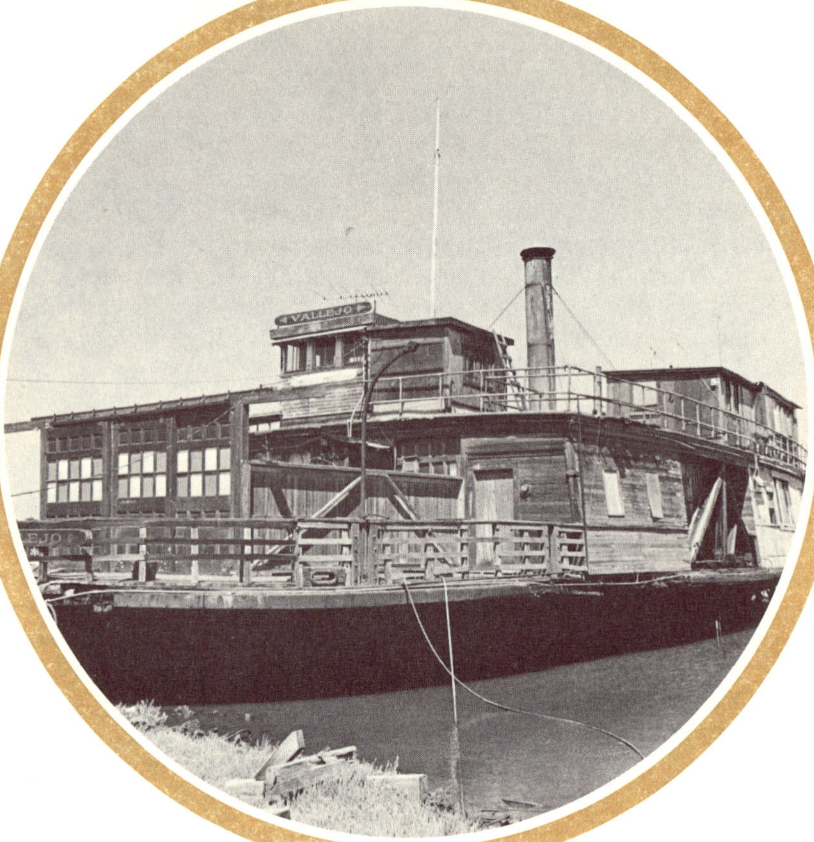
VALLEJO

My home is aboard the ferryboat Vallejo which is tied up at the north end of Sausalito close to San Francisco. You may think a ferryboat is a rather weird place to live. But I've always loved weird things. When I was a little boy, people used to say to me, "Alan, you're so weird. Why can't you be like other people?" I thought that was just plain dull, like having the same thing for dinner every day. And, it is well said, variety is the spice of life.

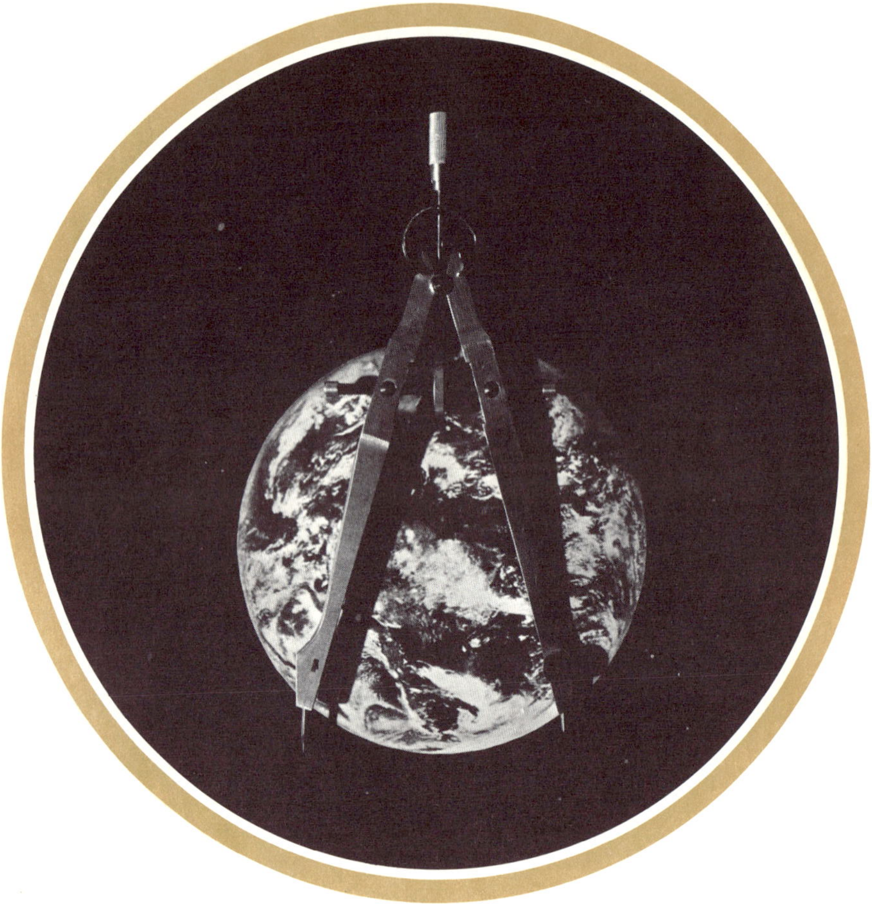

Some things are weird because they are obvious—nobody ever thinks of them. Some of the most fascinating scientific discoveries have been made by people who questioned what was accepted as common sense. Like "Anybody can see that the earth is flat and people know it's flat." The questioning of that fundamental assumption was the beginning of geography.

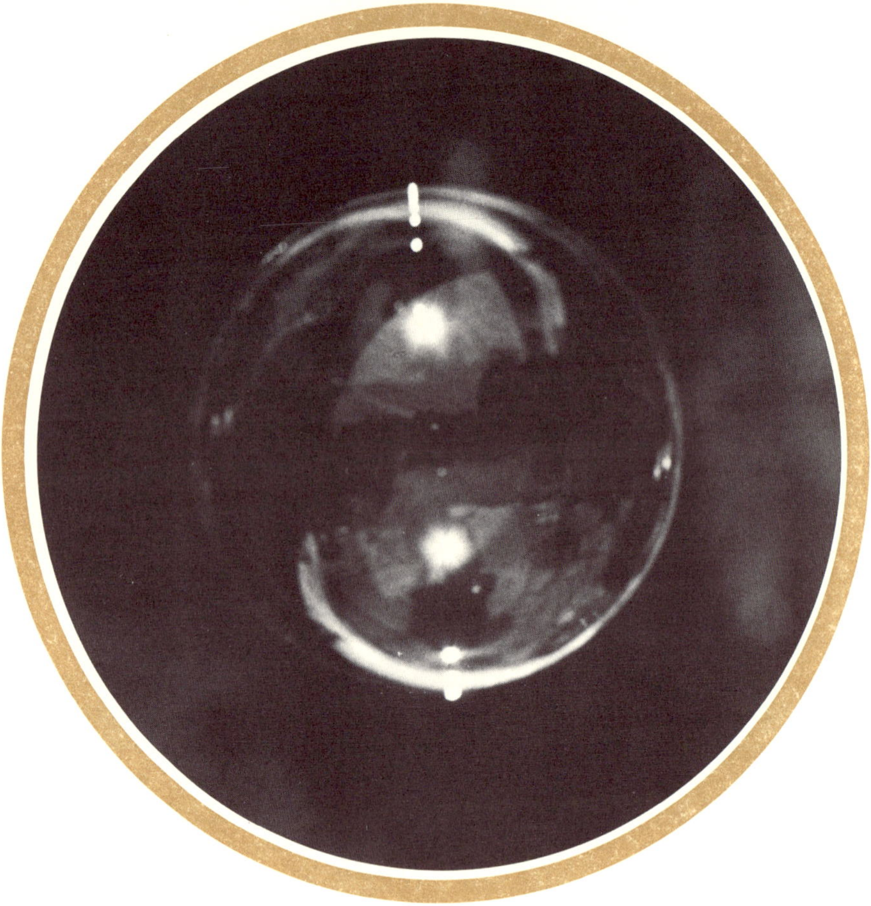

When I consider the weirdest of all things I can think of, do you know what it is? *Nothing*. The whole idea of nothing is something that has bugged people for centuries, especially in the Western world. We have a saying in Latin, *Ex nihilo nihil fit*, which means, "Out of nothing comes nothing." In other words, you can't get something out of nothing. It's occurred to me that this is a fallacy of tremendous proportions. It lies at the root of all our common sense, not only in the West, but in many parts of the East as well. It manifests as a kind of terror of nothing, a putdown on nothing, a putdown on everything associated with nothing such as sleep, passivity, rest, and even the feminine principle which is often equated with the negative principle (although women's lib people don't like that kind of thing, when they understand what I'm saying I don't think they'll object). To me, nothing—the negative, the empty—is exceedingly powerful. I would say, not *Ex nihilo nihil fit*, but, "You can't have something without nothing."

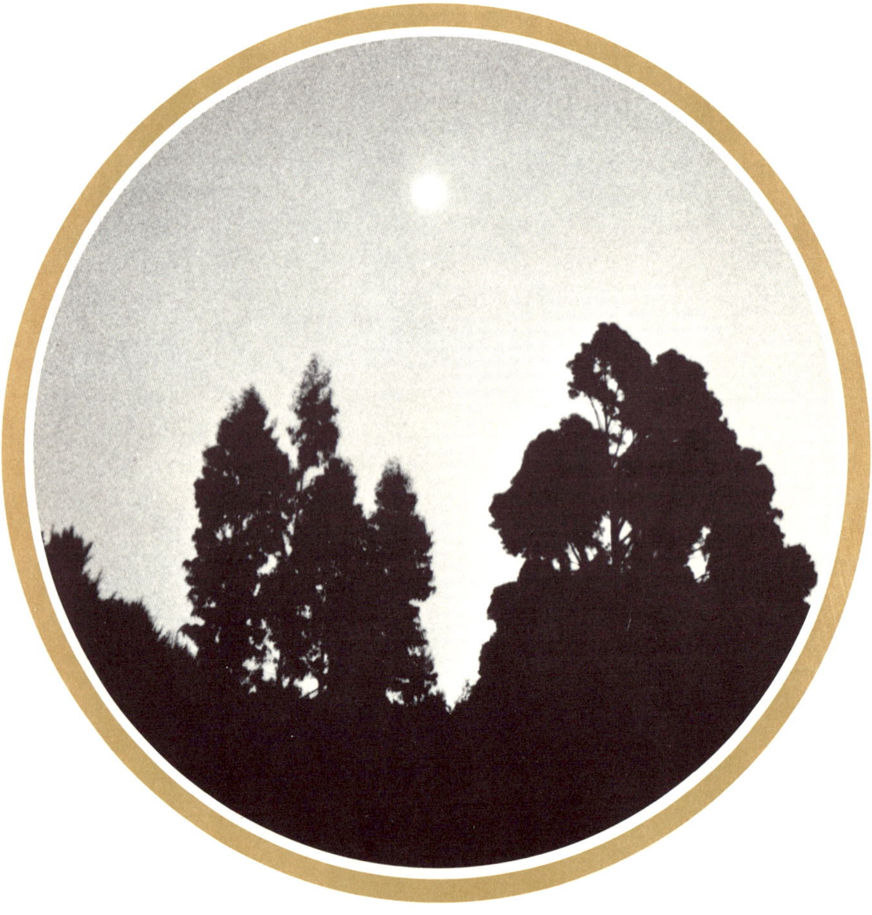

How do we basically begin to think about the difference between something and nothing? When I say there is a cigar in my right hand and there is no cigar in my left hand, we get the idea of *is*, something, and *isn't*, nothing. At the basis of this reasoning lies the far more obvious contrast of solid and space. We tend to think of space as nothing; when we talk about the conquest of space there's a little element of hostility. But actually, we're talking about the conquest of distance. Space or whatever it is that lies between the earth and the moon, and the earth and the sun, is considered to be just nothing at all.

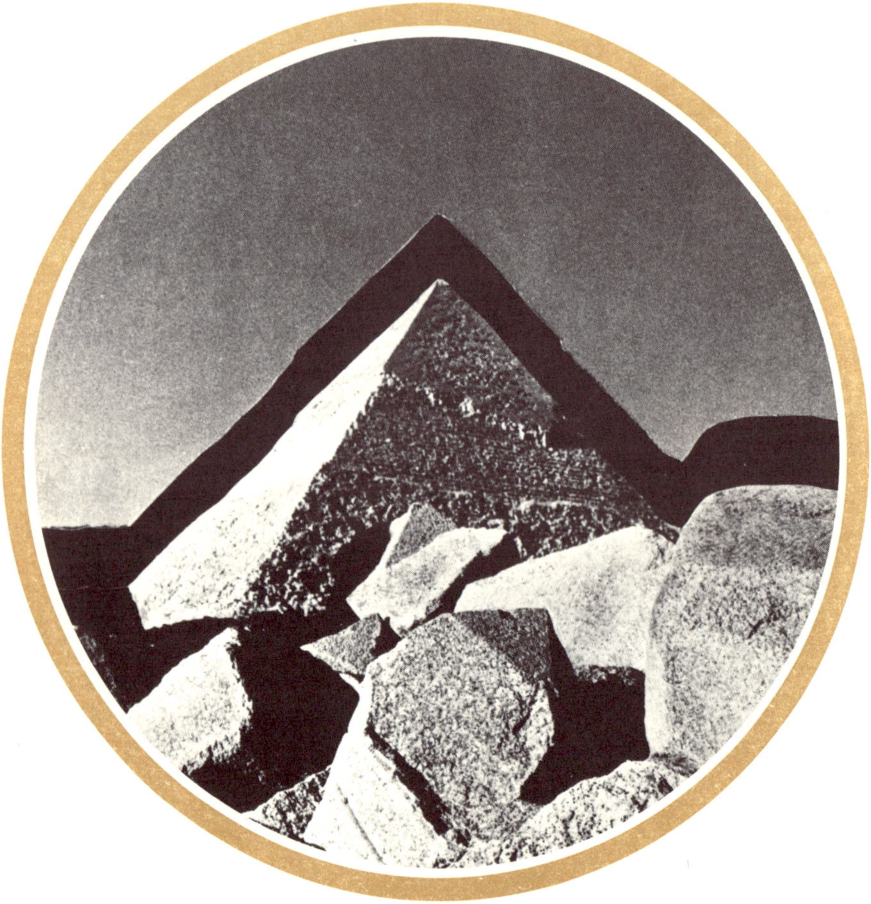

But to suggest how very powerful and important this nothing at all is, let me point out that if you didn't have space, you couldn't have anything solid. Without space outside the solid you wouldn't know where the solid's edges were. For example, you can see me in a photograph because you see a background and that background shows up my outline. But if it weren't there, then I and everything around me would merge into a single, rather peculiar mass. You always have to have a background of space to see a figure. The figure and the background, the solid and the space, are inseparable and go together.

Bering Sea
ALEUTIAN ISLANDS
SHUMAGIN IS
Bristol Bay
Gulf of Alaska
BRITISH
COLUMBIA
ALBERTA
NORTHWEST
SASKATCHEWAN
OREGON
VANCOUVER
C. Scott
C. Flattery
C. Mendocino
San Francisco
Sunday
Saturday

We find this very commonly in the phenomenon of magnetism. A magnet has a north pole and a south pole— there is no such thing as a magnet with one pole only. Supposing we equate north with *is* and south with *isn't*. You can chop the magnet into two pieces, if it's a bar magnet, and just get another north pole and south pole, another *is* and *isn't*, on the end of each piece.

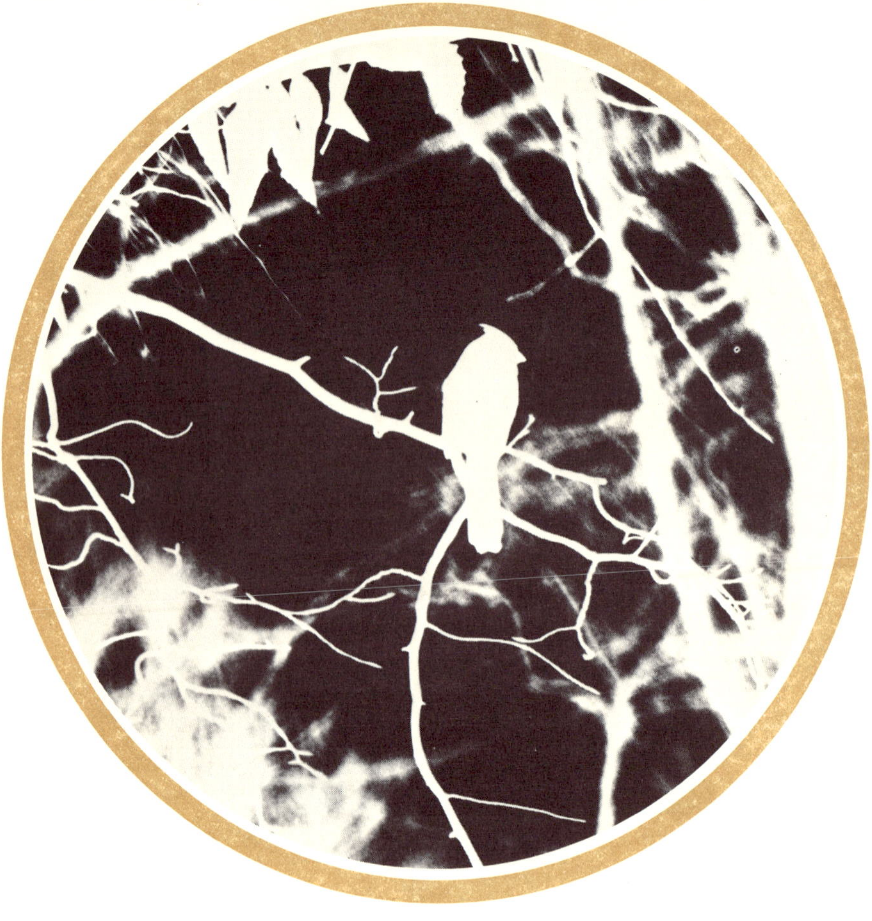

What I am trying to get into basic logic is that there isn't a sort of fight between something and nothing. Everyone is familiar with the famous words of Hamlet, "To be or not to be, that is the question." It isn't; to be or not to be is not the question. Because you can't have a solid without space. You can't have an *is* without an *isn't*, a something without a nothing, a figure without a background. And we can turn that round, and say, "You can't have space without solid."

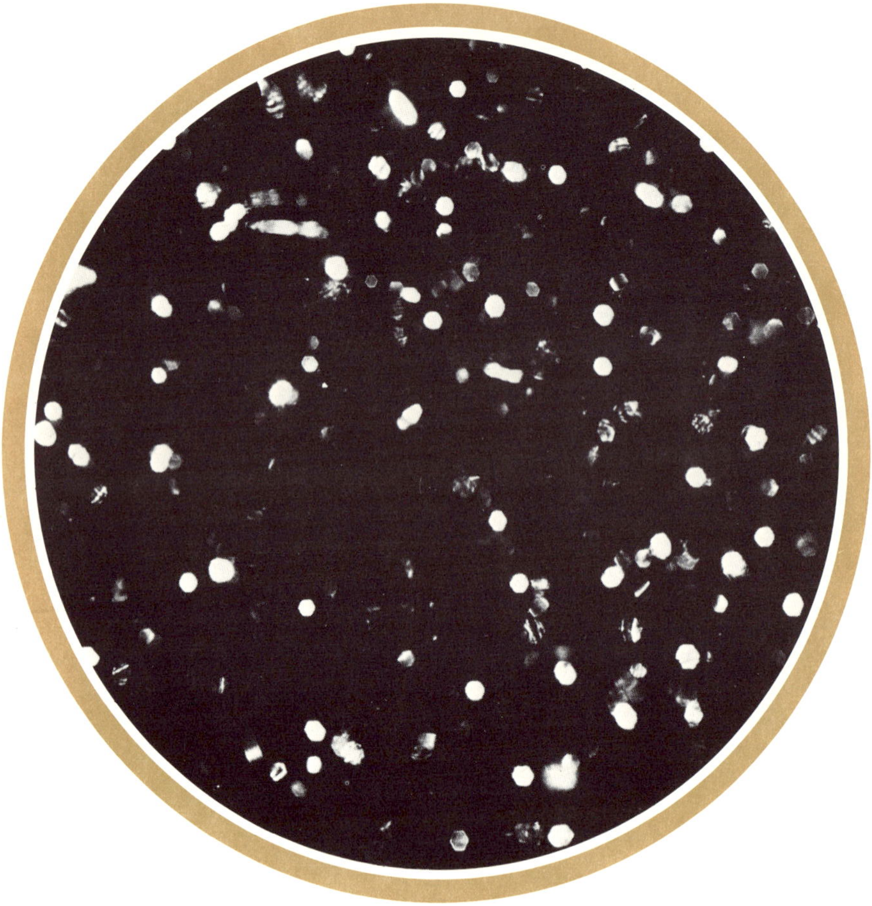

Imagine nothing but space, space, space, space with nothing in it, forever. But there you are imagining it and you're something in it. The whole idea of there being only space, and nothing else at all, is not only inconceivable but perfectly meaningless, because we always know what we mean by contrast.

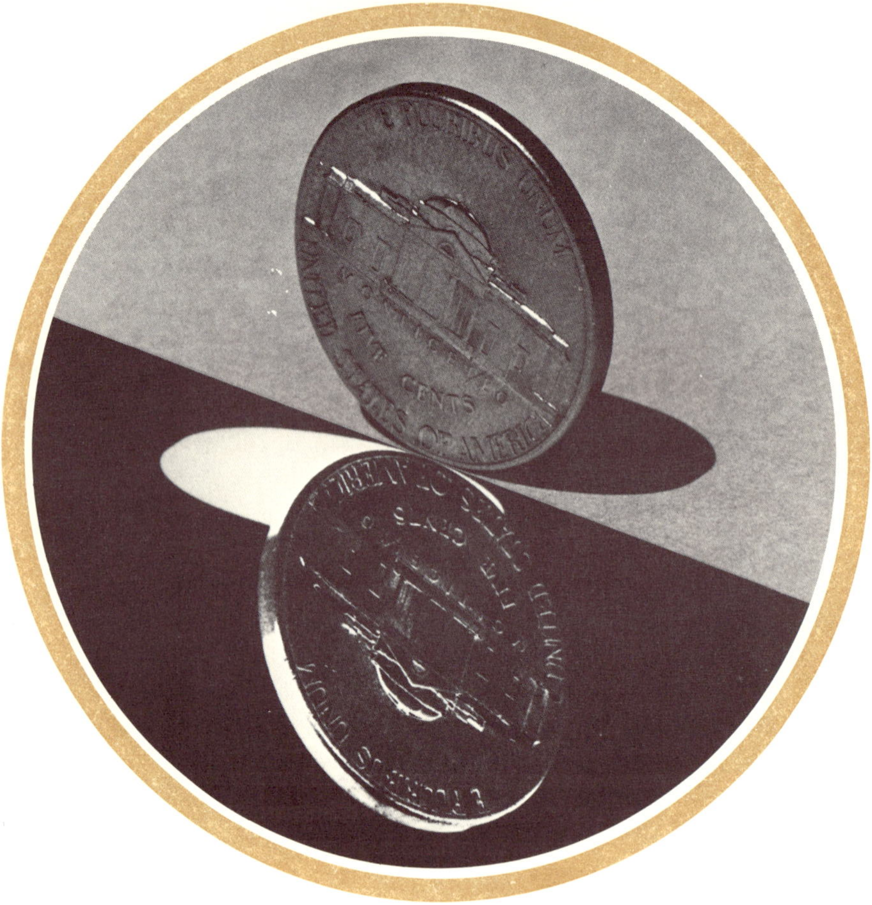
PLURIBUS UNUM
UNITED
FIVE
CENTS
STATES OF AMERICA

We know what we mean by white in comparison with black. We know life in comparison with death. We know pleasure in comparison with pain, up in comparison with down. But all these things must come into being together. You don't have first something and then nothing or first nothing and then something. Something and nothing are two sides of the same coin. If you file away the tails side of a coin completely, the heads side of it will disappear as well. So in this sense, the positive and negative, the something and the nothing, are inseparable—they go together. The nothing is the force whereby the something can be manifested.

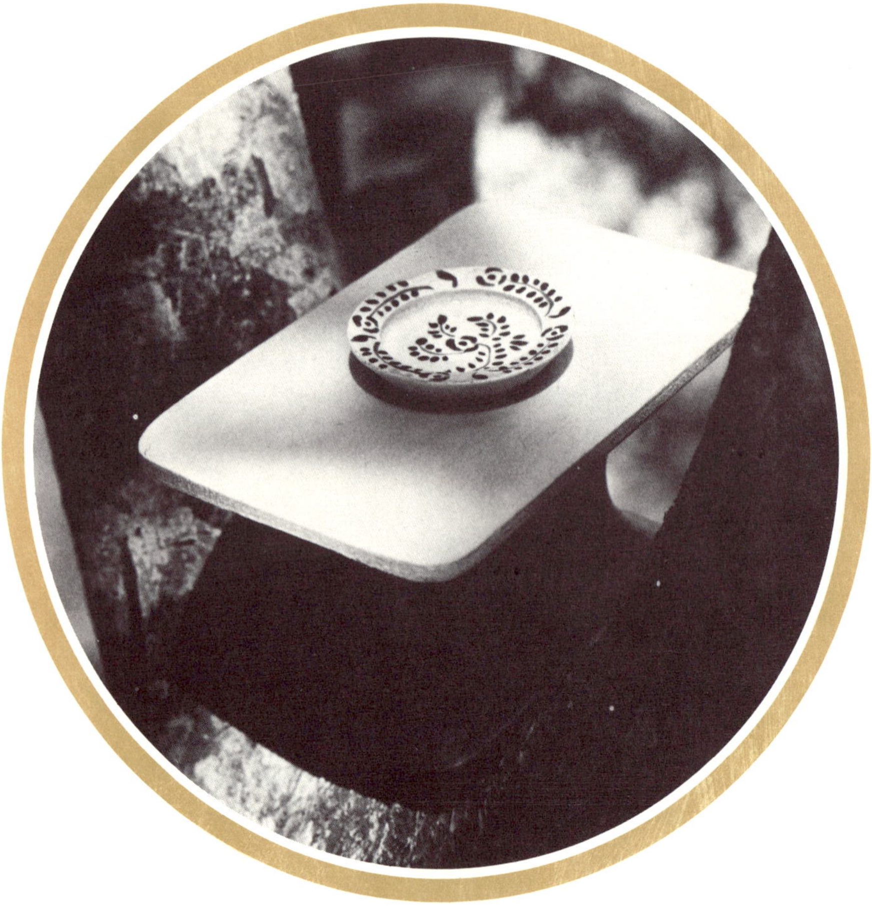

We think that matter is basic to the physical world. And matter has various shapes. We think of tables as made of wood as we think of pots as made of clay. But is a tree made of wood in the same way a table is? No, a tree *is* wood; it isn't *made* of wood. Wood and tree are two different names for the same thing.

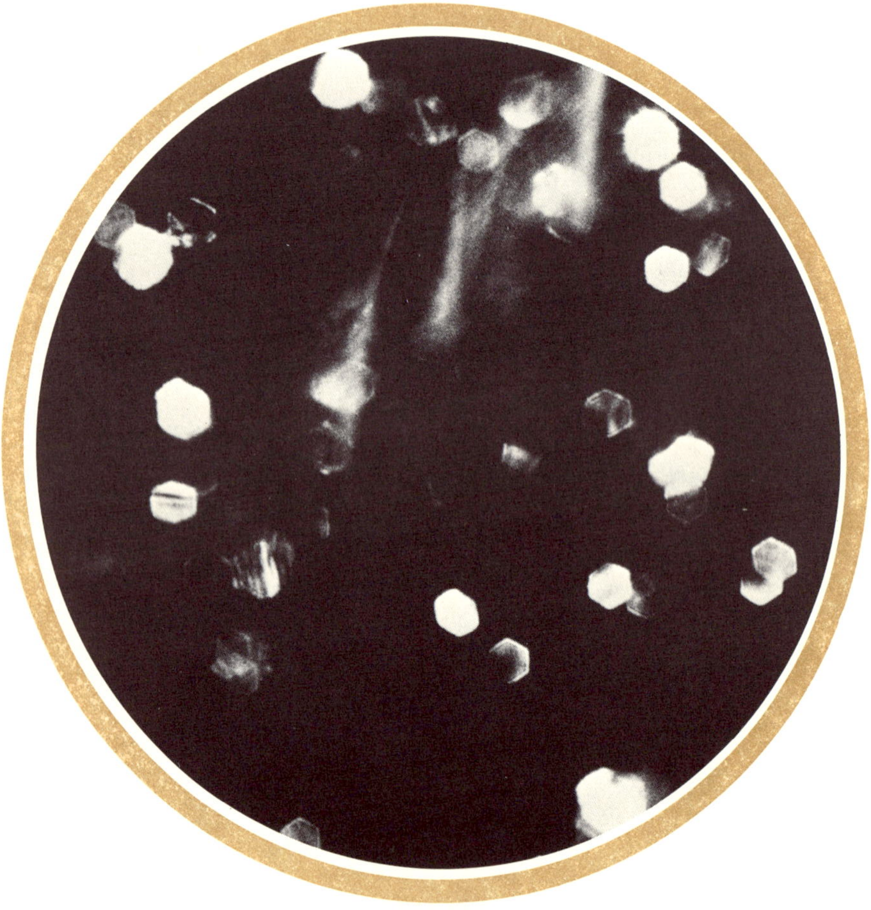

But there is in the back of our mind, the notion, as a root of common sense, that everything in the world is made of some kind of basic *stuff*. Physicists, through centuries, have wanted to know what that was. Indeed, physics began as a quest to discover the basic stuff out of which the world is made. And with all our advances in physics we've never found it. What we have found is not stuff but form. We have found shapes. We have found structures. When you turn up the microscope and look at things expecting to see some sort of stuff, you find instead form, pattern, structure. You find the shape of crystals, beyond the shapes of crystals you find molecules, beyond molecules you find atoms, beyond atoms you find electrons and positrons between which there are vast spaces. We can't decide whether these electrons are waves or particles and so we call them wavicles.

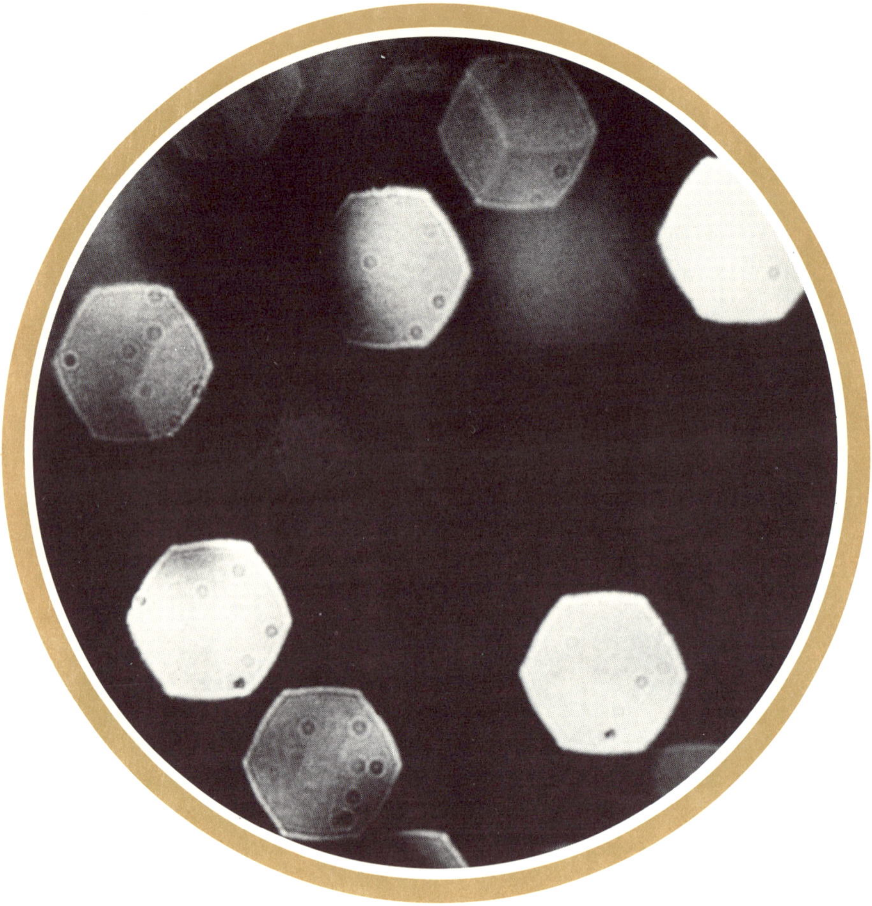

What we will come up with will never be stuff, it will always be a pattern. This pattern can be described, measured, but we never get to any stuff for the simple reason there isn't any. Actually, stuff is when you see something unclearly or out of focus, fuzzy. When we look at it with the naked eye it looks just like goo. We can't make out any significant shape to it. But when you put it under the microscope, you suddenly see shapes. It comes into clear focus as shape.

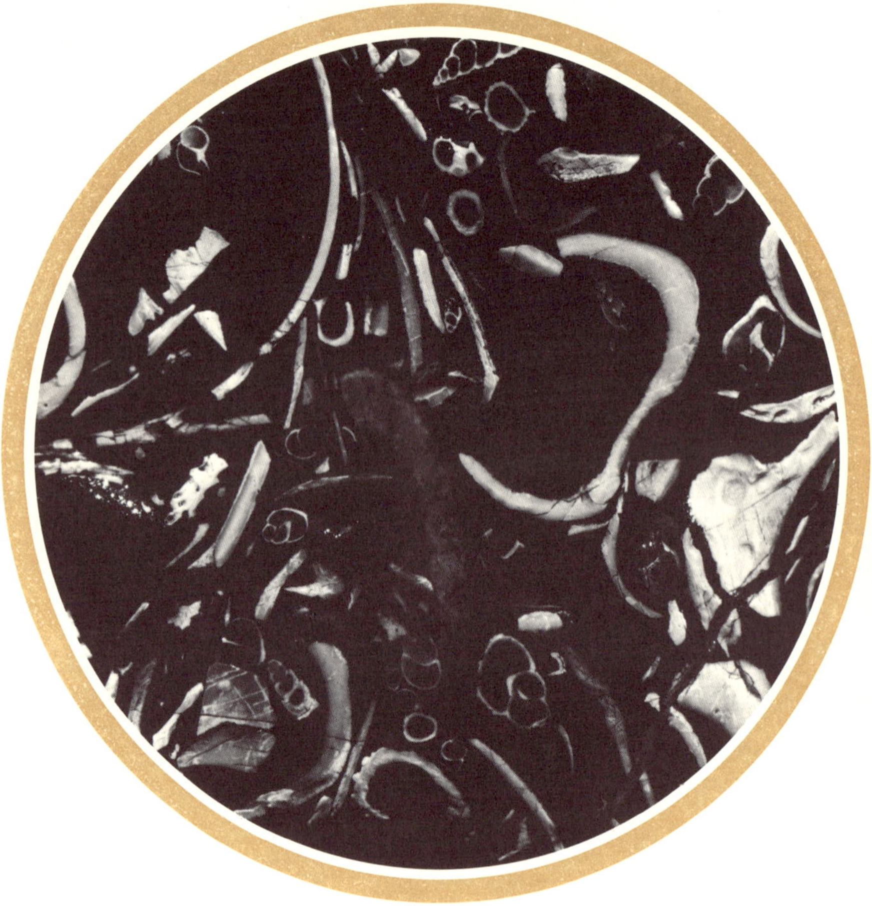

And you can go on and on, looking into the nature of the world and you will never find anything except form. Think of stuff; basic substance. You wouldn't know how to talk about it; even if you found it, how would you describe what it was like? You couldn't say anything about a structure in it, you couldn't say anything about a pattern or a process in it, because it would be absolute, primordial goo.

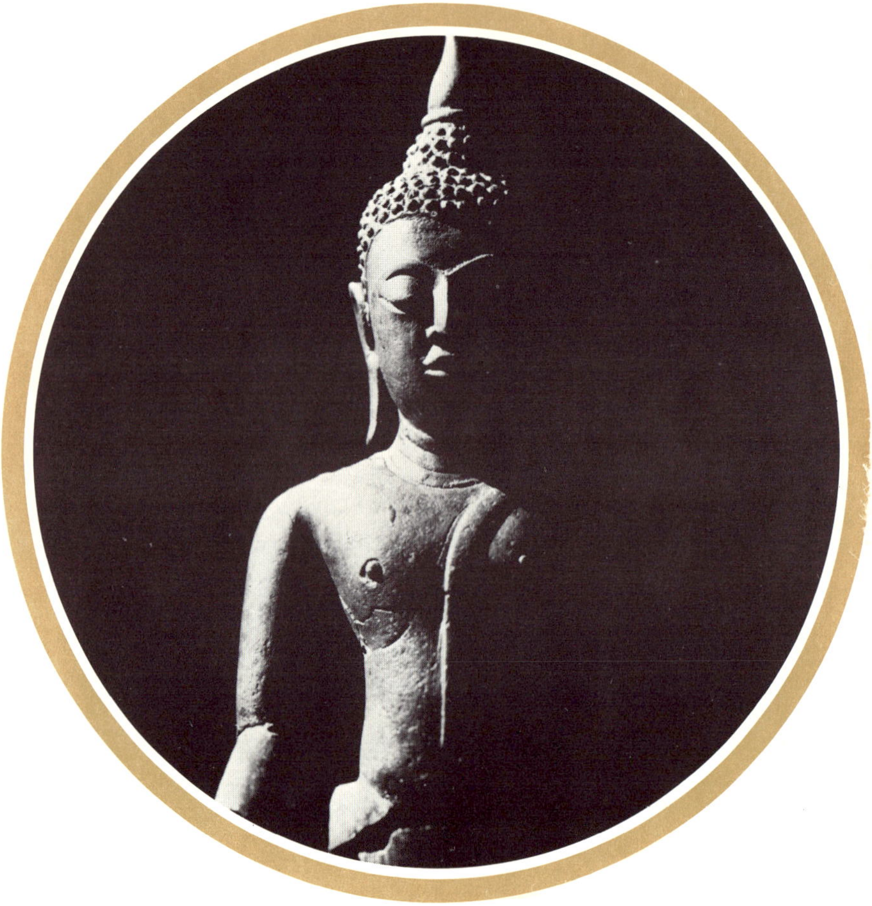

What else is there besides form in the world? Obviously, between the significant shapes of any form there is space. And space and form go together as the fundamental things we're dealing with in this universe. The whole of Buddhism is based on a saying, "That which is void is precisely form, and that which is form is precisely void." Let me illustrate this to you in an extremely simple way. When you use the word *clarity*, what do you mean? It might mean a perfectly polished lens, or mirror, or a clear day when there's no smog and the air is perfectly transparent like space.

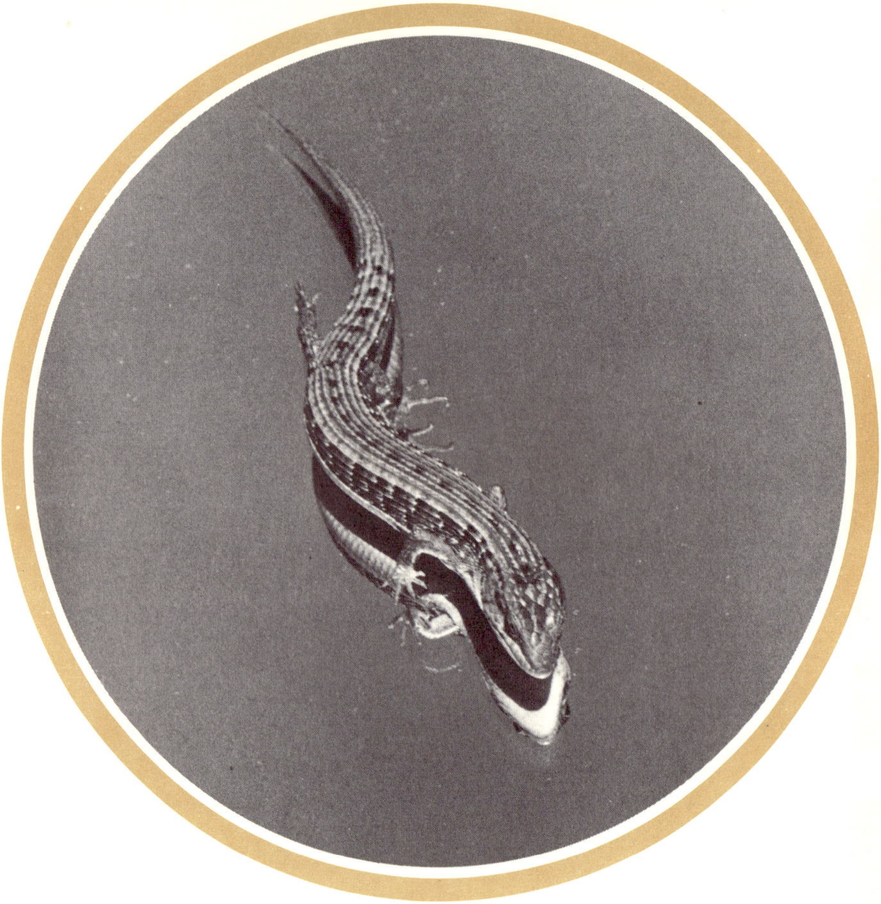

What's the next thing *clarity* makes you think of? You think of form in clear focus, all the details articulate and perfect. So the one word *clarity* suggests to you these two apparently completely different things: the clarity of the lens or the mirror, and the clarity of articulate form. In this sense, we can take the saying "Form is void, void is form" and instead of saying *is*, say *implies*, or the word that I invented *goeswith*. Form always goeswith void. And there really isn't, in this whole universe, any substance.

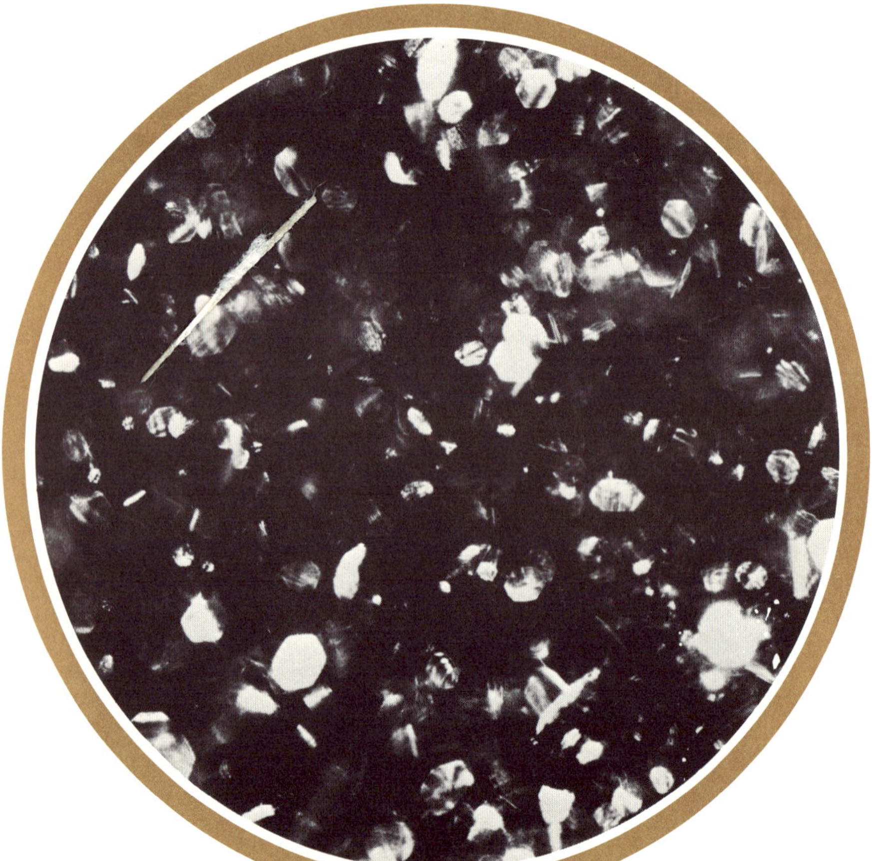

Form, indeed, is inseparable from the idea of energy, and form, especially when it's moving in a very circumscribed area, appears to us as solid. For example, when you spin an electric fan the empty spaces between the blades sort of disappear into a blur, and you can't push a pencil, much less your finger, through the fan. So in the same way, you can't push your finger through the floor because the floor's going too fast. Basically, what you have down there is nothing and form in motion.

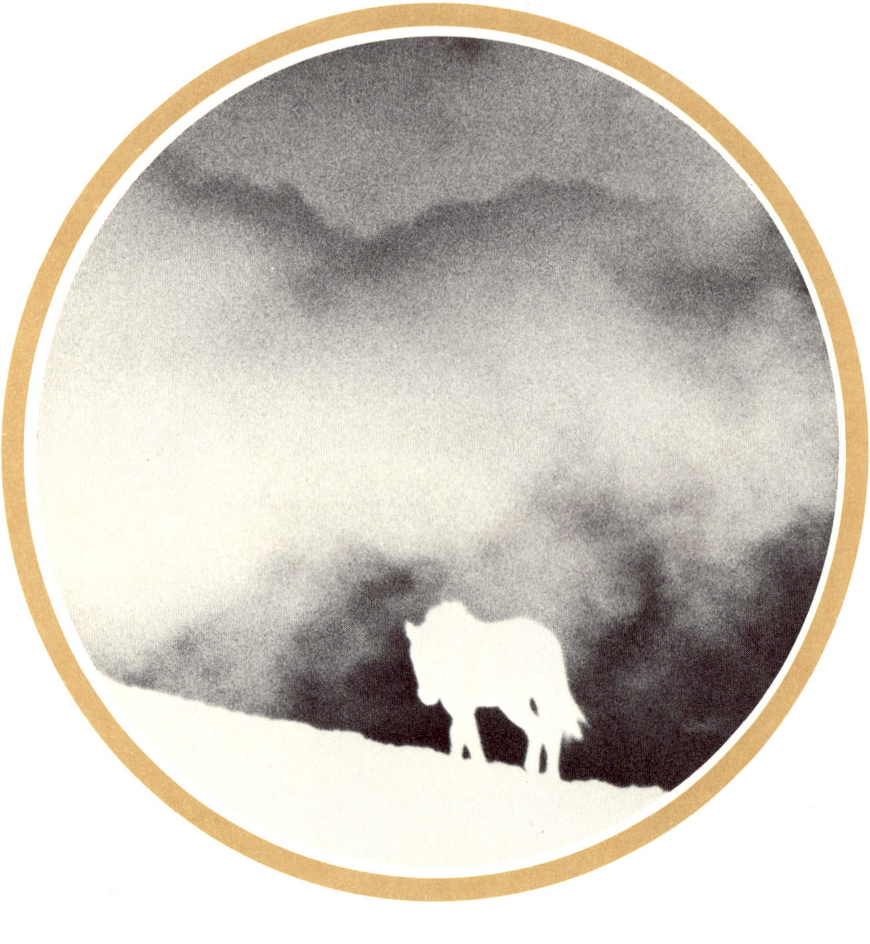

I knew of a physicist at the University of Chicago who was rather crazy like some scientists, and the idea of the insolidity, the instability of the physcial world, impressed him so much that he used to go around in enormous padded slippers for fear he should fall through the floor. So this commonsense notion that the world is made of some kind of substance is a nonsense idea—it isn't there at all but is, instead, form and emptiness.

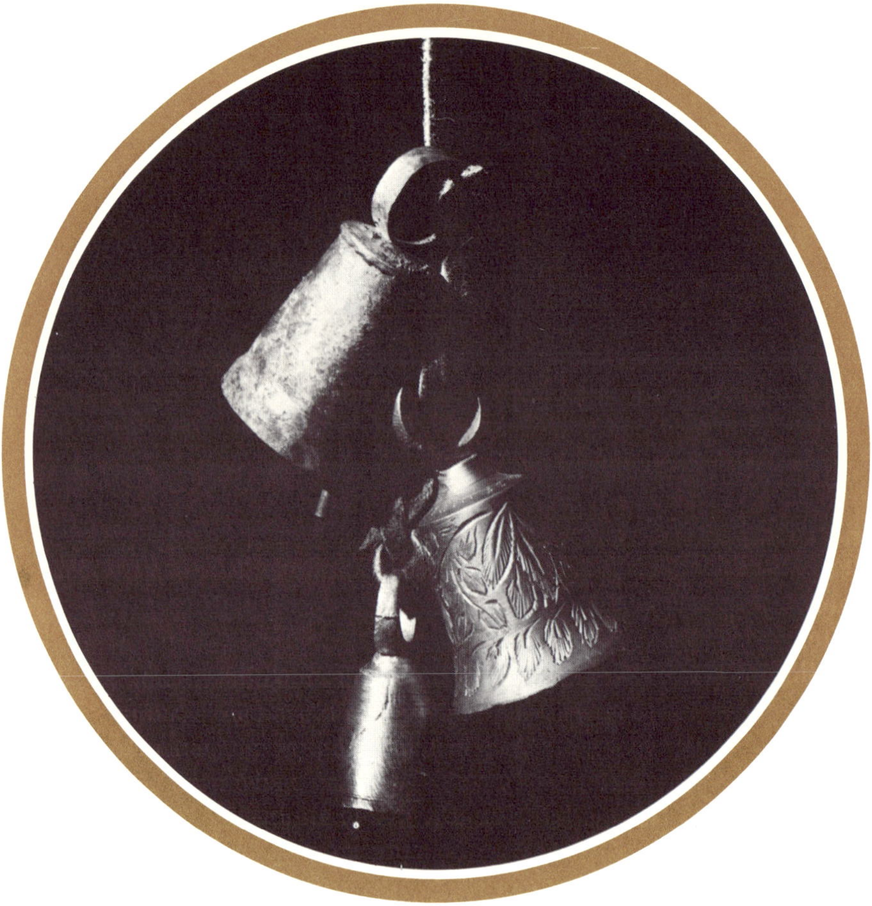

Most forms of energy are vibration, pulsation. The energy of light or the energy of sound are always on and off. In the case of very fast light, very strong light, even with alternating current you don't notice the discontinuity because your retina retains the impression of the *on* pulse and you can't notice the *off* pulse except in very slow light like an arc lamp. It's exactly the same thing with sound. A high note seems more continuous because the vibrations are faster than a low note. In the low note you hear a kind of graininess because of the slower alternations of on and off.

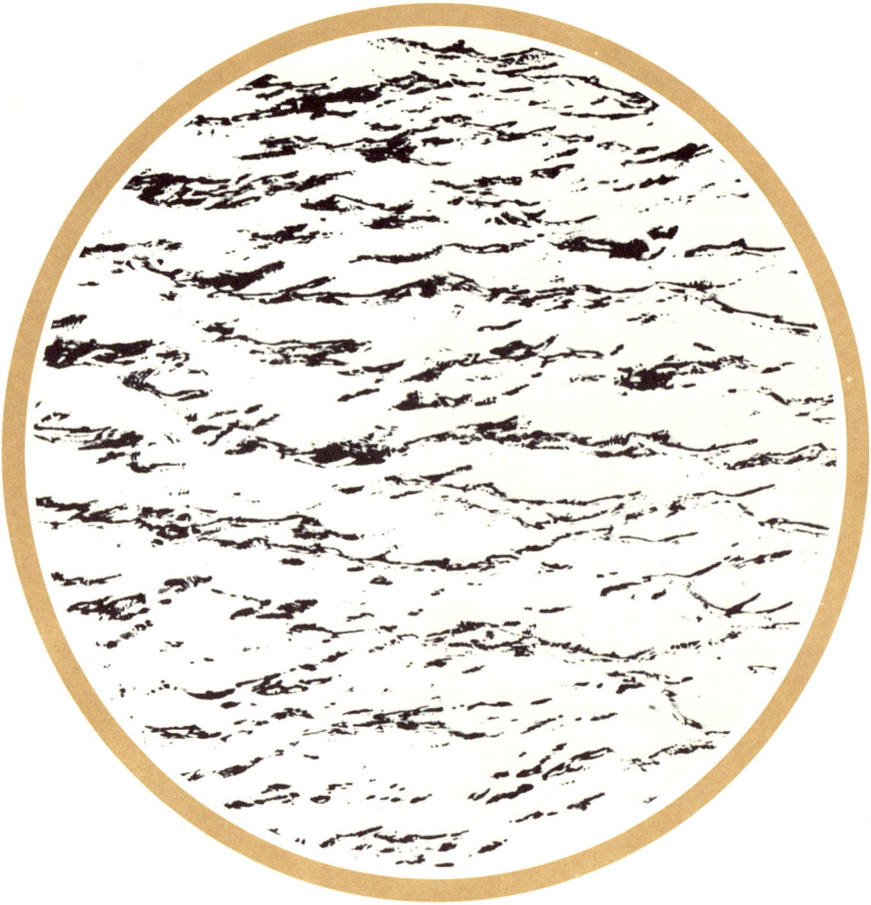

All wave motion is this process, and when we think of waves, we think about crests. The crests stand out from the underlying, uniform bed of water. These crests are perceived as the things, the forms, the waves. But you cannot have the emphasis called a crest, the concave, without the de-emphasis, or convex, called the trough. So to have anything standing out, there must be something standing down or standing back. We must realize that if you had this part alone, the up part, that would not excite your senses because there would be no contrast.

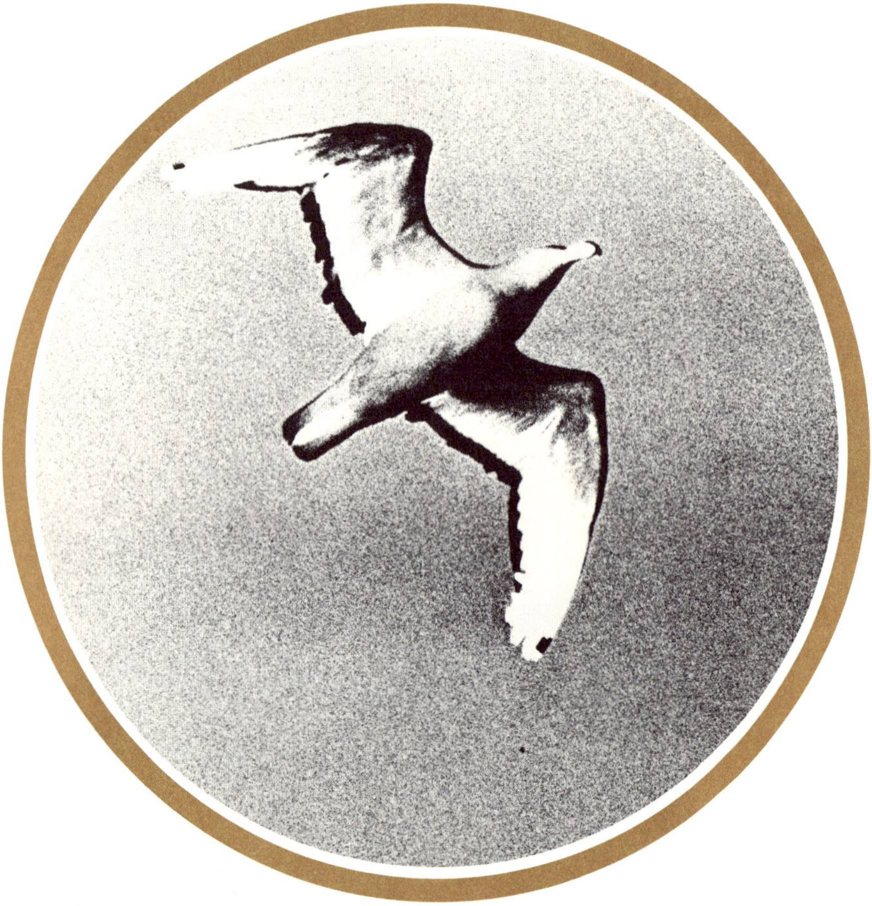

The same thing is true of all life together. We shouldn't really contrast existence with nonexistence, because actually, existence is the alternation of now-you-see-it/now-you-don't, now-you-see-it/now-you-don't, now-you-see-it/now-you-don't. It is that contrast that presents the sensation of there being anything at all.

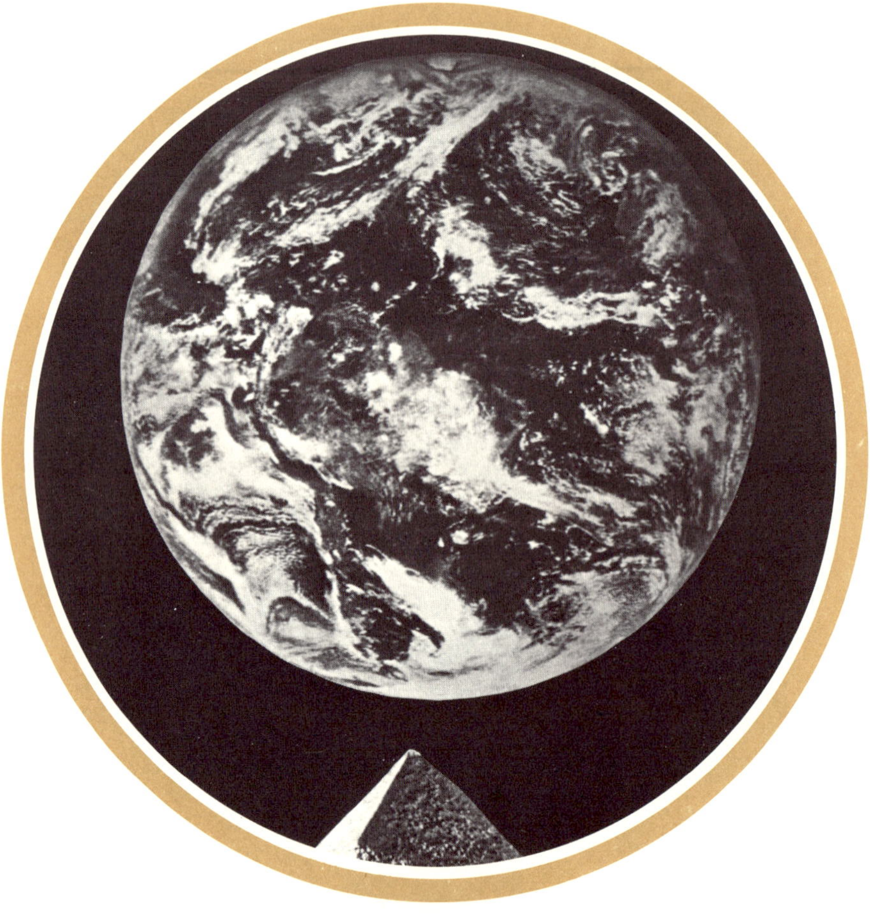

Now, in light and sound the waves are extraordinarily rapid so that we don't hear or see the interval between them. But there are other circumstances in which the waves are extraordinarily slow, as in the alternation of day and night, light and darkness, and the much vaster alternations of life and death. But these alternations are just as necessary to the being of the universe as in the very fast motions of light and sound, and in the sense of solid contact when it's going so rapidly that we notice only continuity or the *is* side. We ignore the intervention of the *isn't* side, but it's there just the same, just as there are vast spaces within the very heart of the atom.

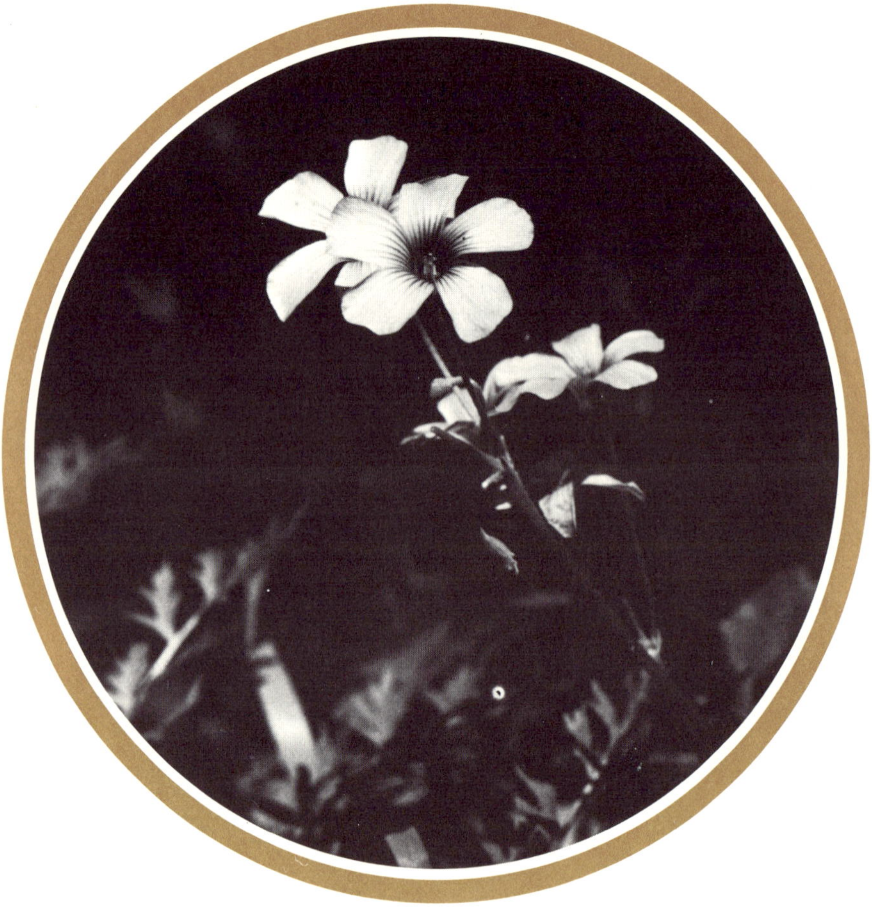

Another thing that goes along with all this is that it's perfectly obvious that the universe is a system which is aware of itself. In other words, we, as living organisms, are forms of the energy of the universe just as much as the stars and the galaxies, and, through our sense organs, this system of energy becomes aware of itself.

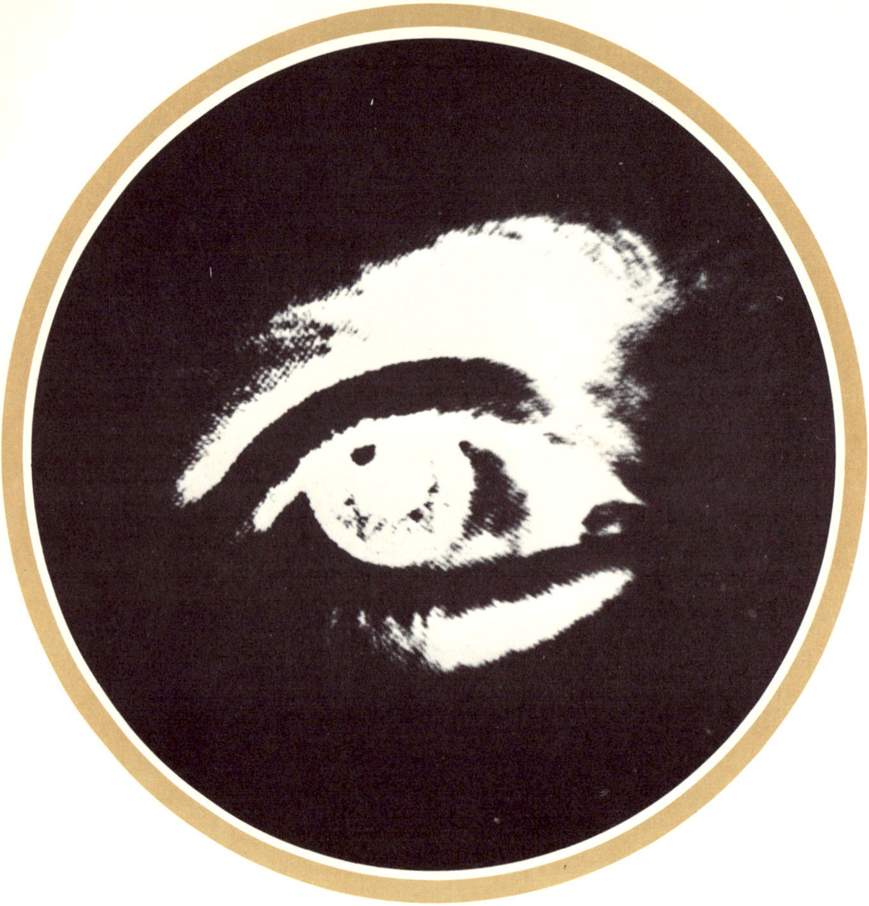

But to understand this we must again relate back to our basic contrast between on and off, something and nothing, which is that the aspect of the universe which is aware of itself, which does the awaring, does not see itself. In other words, you can't look at your eyes with your eyes. You can't observe yourself in the act of observing. You can't touch the tip of a finger with the tip of the same finger no matter how hard you try. Therefore, there is on the reverse side of all observation a blank spot; for example, behind your eyes from the point of view of your eyes. However you look around there is blankness behind them. That's unknown. That's the part of the universe which does not see itself because it is seeing.

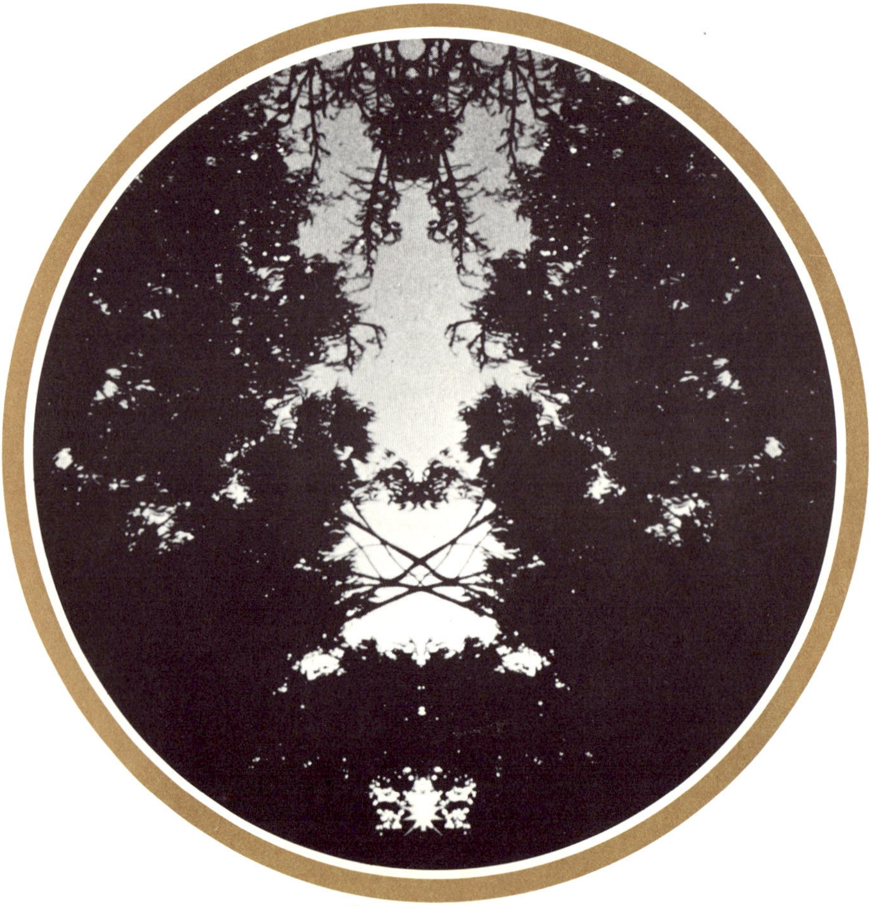

We always get this division of experience into one-half known, one-half unknown. We would like to know, if we could, this always unknown. If we examine the brain and the structure of the nerves behind the eyes, we're always looking at somebody else's brain. We're never able to look at our own brain at the same time we're investigating somebody else's brain.

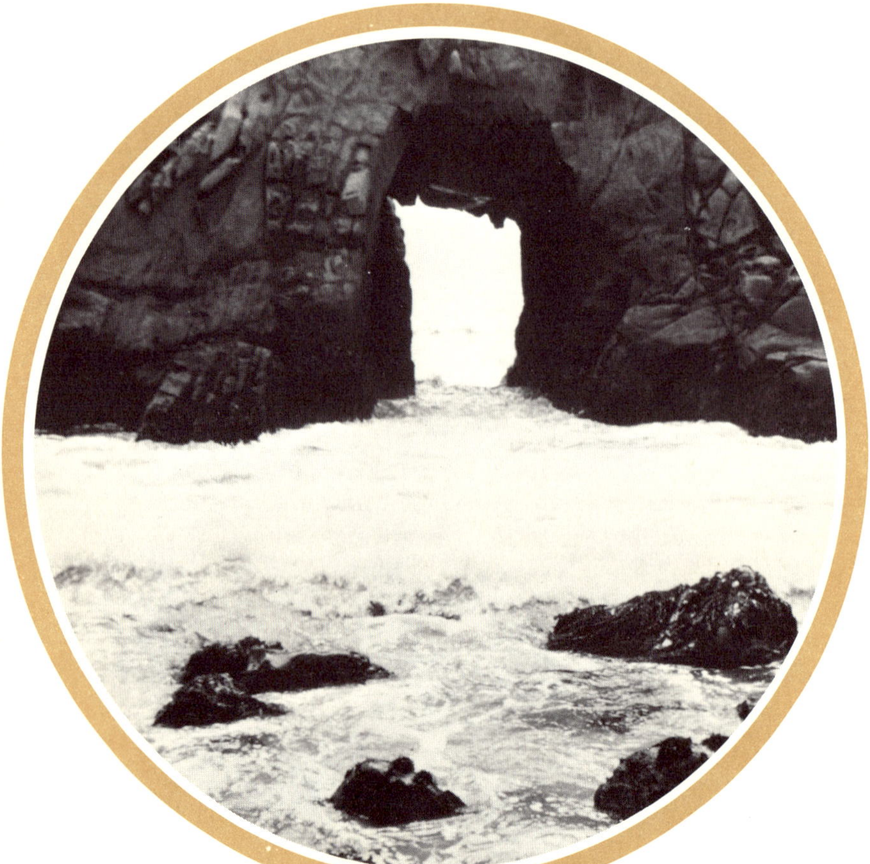

So there is always this blank side of experience. What I'm suggesting is that the blank side of experience has the same relationship to the conscious side as the *off* principle of vibration has to the *on* principle. There's a fundamental division. The Chinese call them the *yang*, the positive side, and the *yin*, the negative side. This corresponds to the idea of one and zero. All numbers can be made of one and zero as in the binary system of numbers which is used for computers.

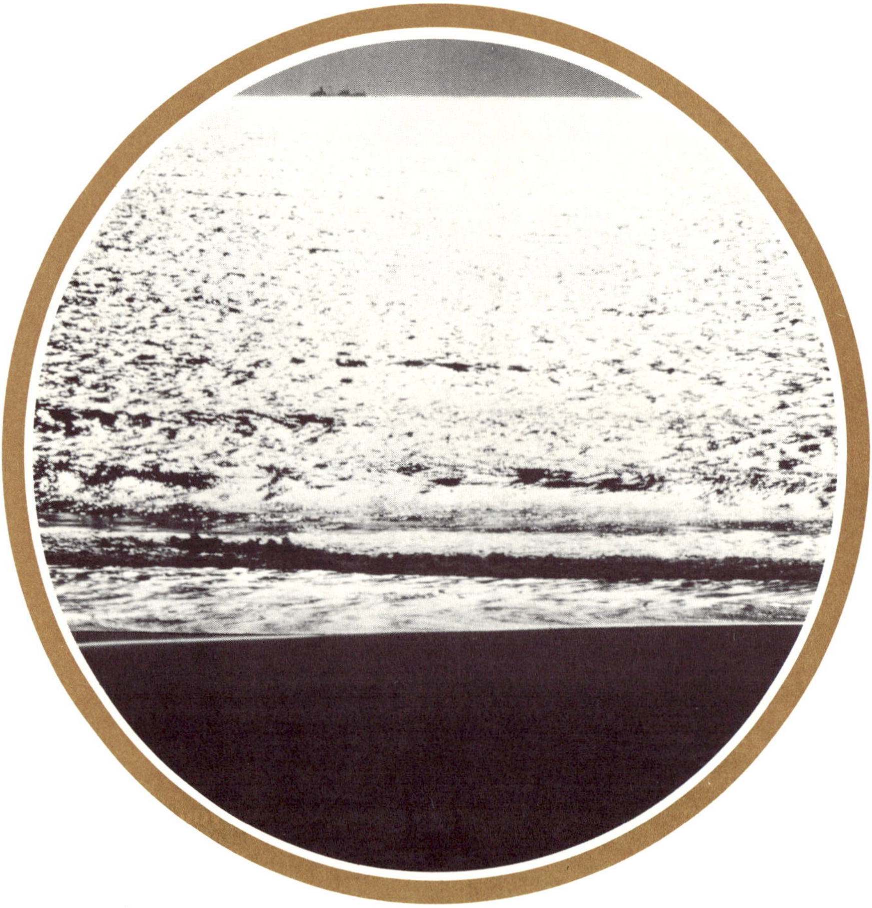

And so it's all made up of off and on, and conscious and unconscious. But the unconscious is the part of experience which is doing consciousness, just as the trough manifests the wave, the space manifests the solid, the background manifests the figure. And so all that side of life which you call unconscious, unknown, impenetrable, *is* unconscious, unknown, impenetrable because it's really you. In other words, the deepest you is the nothing side, is the side which you don't know.

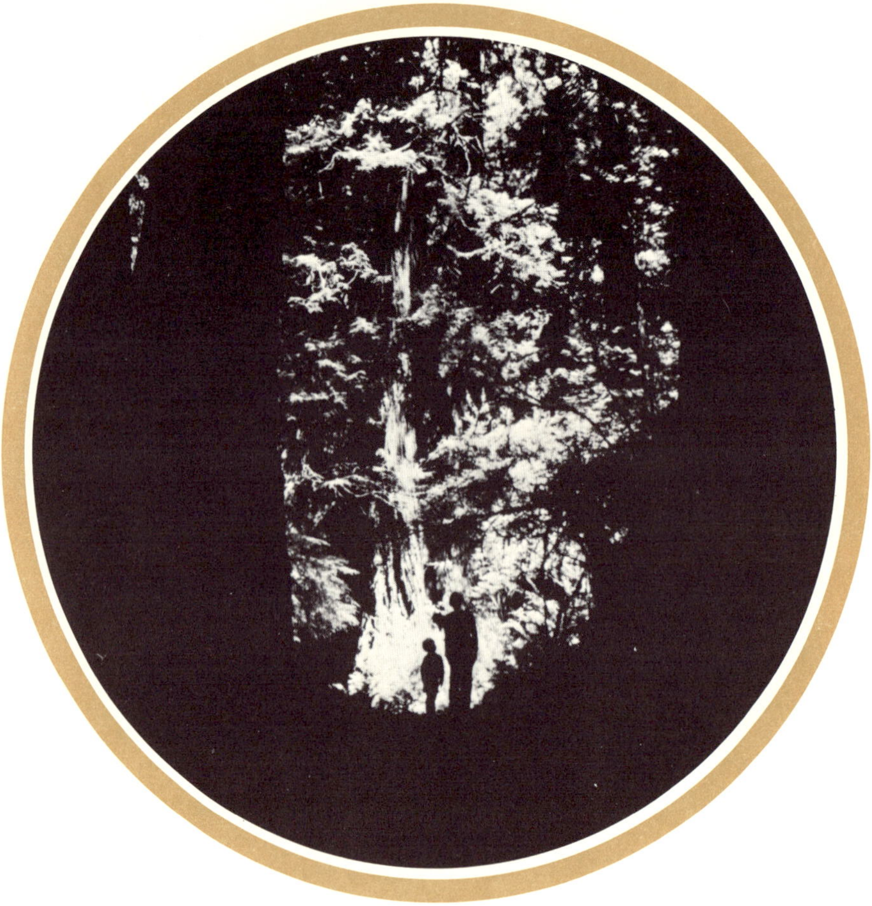

So, don't be afraid of nothing. I could say, "There's nothing in nothing to be afraid of." But people in our culture are terrified of nothing. They're terrified of death; they are uneasy about sleep, because they think it's a waste of time. They have a lurking fear in the back of their minds that the universe is eventually going to run down and end in nothing, and it will all be forgotten, buried and dead. But this is a completely unreasonable fear, because it is just precisely this nothing which is always the source of something.

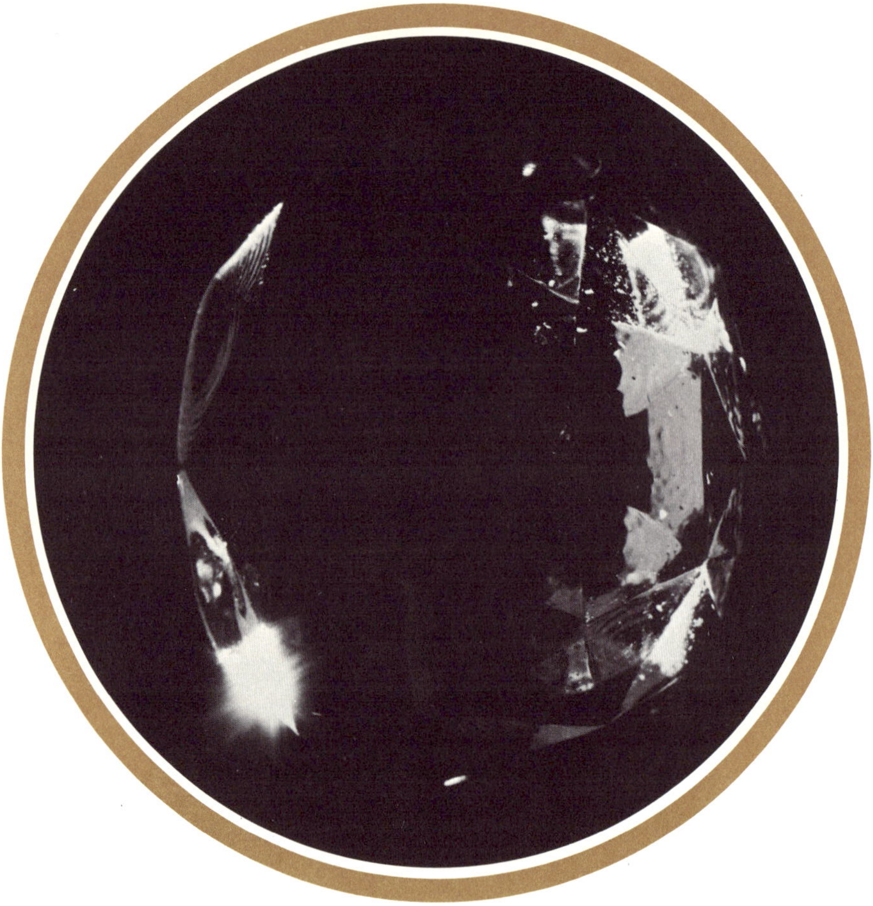

Think once again of the image of clarity, crystal clear. *Nothing* is what brings *something* into focus. This *nothing*, symbolized by the crystal, is your own eyeball, your own consciousness.

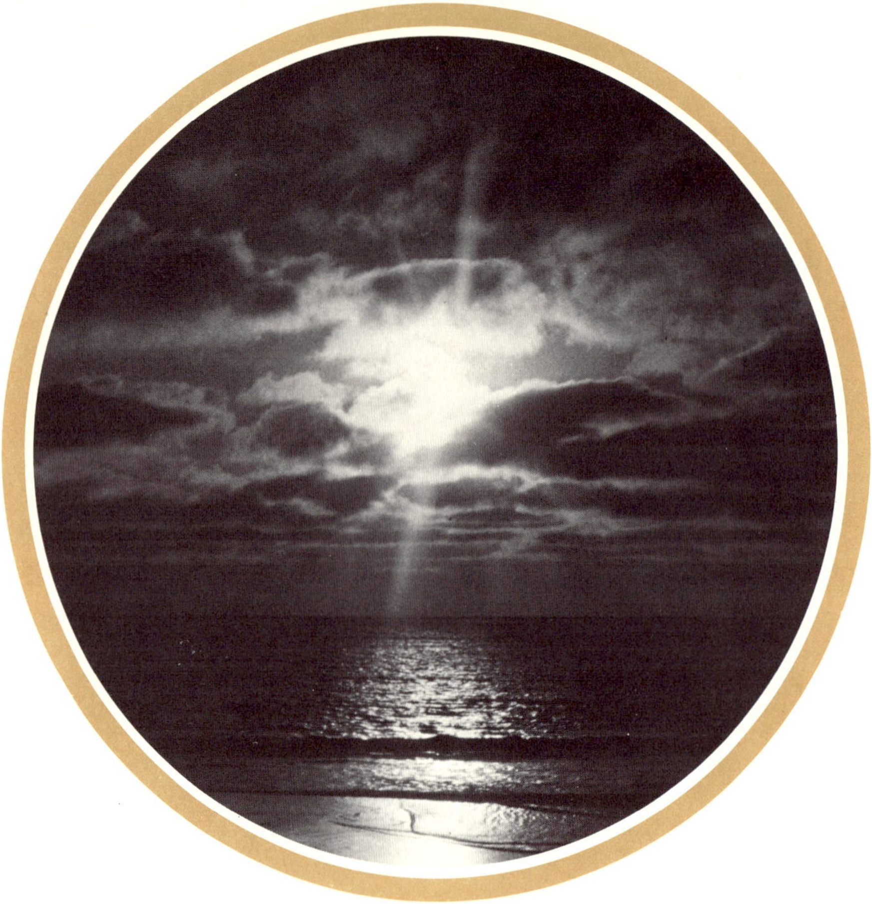

OTHER BOOKS by ALAN WATTS

The Spirit of Zen
The Meaning of Happiness
The Theologia Mystica of St. Dionvsius
Behold the Spirit
The Supreme Identity
The Wisdom of Insecurity
Myth and Ritual in Christianity
The Way of Liberation in Zen Buddhism
The Way of Zen
Nature, Man, and Woman
This Is It
Psychotherapy East and West
The Joyous Cosmology
The Two Hands of God
Beyond Theology: The Art of Godmanship
Nonsense
The Book: On the Taboo Against Knowing Who You Are
Does It Matter? Essays on Man's Relation to Materiality
Erotic Spirituality
In My Own Way: An Autobiography
The Art of Contemplation

To order tapes of Alan Watts' lectures, send for a free catalog to:
EU, Box 361, Mill Valley, California 94941

OTHER BOOKS OF INTEREST FROM
CELESTIAL ARTS

THE ESSENCE OF ALAN WATTS. The basic philosophy of Alan Watts in nine illustrated volumes. Now available:
GO
ME
WILL ... uel to You & I. 96 pages, ...

THE HUMANNE... & Vol. ... y rendered in his own words and photographs. Ea... : 64 pages, paper, $2.95.

MY DEAREST FRIEND. The compassion and sensitivity that marked Walt Rinder's previous works are displayed again in this beautiful new volume. 64 pages, paper, $2.95.

ONLY ONE TODAY. Walt Rinder's widely acclaimed style is again apparent in this beautifully illustrated poem. 64 pages, paper, $2.95

THE HEALING MIND by Dr. Irving Oyle. A noted physician describes what is known about the mysterious ability of the mind to heal the body. 128 pages, cloth, $7.95; paper, $4.95.

I WANT TO BE USED not abused by Ed Branch. How to adapt to the demands of others and gain more pleasure from relationships. 80 pages, paper, $2.95.

INWARD JOURNEY Art and Psychotherapy For You by Margaret Keyes. A therapist demonstrates how anyone can use art as a healing device. 128 pages, paper, $4.95.

PLEASE TRUST ME by James Vaughan. A simple, illustrated book of poetry about the quality too often lacking in our experiences—Trust. 64 pages, paper, $2.95.

LOVE IS AN ATTITUDE. The world-famous book of poetry and photographs by Walter Rinder. 128 pages, cloth, $7.95; paper, $3.95.

THIS TIME CALLED LIFE. Poetry and photography by Walter Rinder. 160 pages, cloth, $7.95; paper, $3.95.

SPECTRUM OF LOVE. Walter Rinder's remarkable love poem with magnificently enhancing drawings by David Mitchell. 64 pages, cloth, $7.95; paper, $2.95.

GROWING TOGETHER. George and Donni Betts' poetry with photographs by Robert Scales. 128 pages, paper, $3.95.

VISIONS OF YOU. Poems by George Betts, with photographs by Robert Scales. 128 pages, paper, $3.95.

MY GIFT TO YOU. New poems by George Betts, with photographs by Robert Scales. 128 pages, paper, $3.95.

YOU & I. Leonard Nimoy, the distinguished actor, blends his poetry and photography into a beautiful love story. 128 pages, cloth, $7.95; paper, $3.95.

I AM. Concepts of awareness in poetic form by Michael Grinder. Illustrated in color by Chantal. 64 pages, paper, $2.95.

GAMES STUDENTS PLAY (And what to do about them.) A study of Transactional Analysis in schools, by Kenneth Ernst. 128 pages, cloth, $7.95; paper, $3.95.

A GUIDE FOR SINGLE PARENTS (Transactional Analysis for People in Crisis.) T.A. for single parents by Kathryn Hallett. 128 pages, cloth, $7.95; paper, $3.95.

THE PASSIONATE MIND (A Manual for Living Creatively with One's Self.) Guidance and understanding from Joel Kramer. 128 pages, paper, $3.95.